VIA FOLIOS 121

SECOND THOUGHTS

Second Thoughts

Dennis Barone

Library of Congress Control Number: 2017939293

Printed in the United States.

Published by
BORDIGHERA PRESS
John D. Calandra Italian American Institute
25 West 43rd Street, 17th Floor
New York, NY 10036

VIA FOLIOS 121
ISBN 978-1-59954-114-3

Furnished Rooms by Emanuel Carnevali (Bordighera, 2006)

Visiting Wallace: Poems Inspired by the Life and Work of Wallace Stevens (with James Finnegan) (University of Iowa, 2009)

Small Towns, Big Cities: The Urban Experience of Italian Americans (with Stefano Luconi) (American Italian Historical Association, 2010)

New Hungers for Old: One-Hundred Years of Italian-American Poetry (Star Cloud, 2011)

Essays on Italian American Literature and Culture (with Peter Covino) (Bordighera, 2012)

Garnet Poems: An Anthology of Connecticut Poetry Since 1776 (Wesleyan University, 2012)

Some of this work appeared in *Freshwater, The Hartford Courant, Italian Americana, The Paterson Literary Review, Voices in Italian Americana,* and *The Wallace Stevens Journal.* "Pass Go and Collect" appeared on-line in *Atlas and Alice,* "Vast Oculus" in *Posit,* and part of "Rope Snake: A Fragment" in *A Festschrift for Tony Frazer.*

COVER: John Willis, *Reconciliation V*, color etching, 2011.

We fancy men are individuals; so are pumpkins; but every pumpkin in the field, goes through every point of pumpkin history.

Ralph Waldo Emerson, "Nominalist and Realist"

TABLE OF CONTENTS

Second Thoughts

DIFFERENCE OF OPINION

They waited for the train, each top-hat slightly askew toward the left. Their crimson ties tight despite the delay; left-hand snug in left-pocket.

They could hear its approach and that sound only made the wait evermore excruciating. And if they should be late?

But sometime later that afternoon they boarded, took their seats, and then anticipated arrival. Who would greet them: the Blues or the Greens? Such did they wonder as the wheels began to turn once more and then turned faster and faster.

And before they knew it, they had arrived at their station. They hadn't had time to order tea or beer. Oh, well — just as well: for soon they had to perform and they felt that this evening would be special for them.

As they left the train a strange bird lighted into a tree near them, a bird such as they had never seen before and they did not know what it meant for them, if anything, for they were not prone to superstition. Instrument cases in hand, they looked up and saw there in that tree looking down upon them that peculiar bird. What could it portend?

They had decided to walk to the concert hall. Neither a Blue nor a Green had arrived to meet them. But the hall wasn't very far, and as they walked that most unusual avian creature followed, hop-scotching tree to tree. The bird seemed to be mocking the orchestra somehow; for some reason.

They were to play the War Symphony this night. Could that be it: the bird, a peacenik?

At the entrance to the hall they paused before entering and looked once more upon the visage of that foreboding creature. From on high it seemed to wink at them and then followed a high pitched whistle that sounded loud and lasted long into the night.

After the concert as they walked toward the station, instruments in one hand and the other snug in a pocket, they could still hear that solitary bird's shrill cry. They knew not what in the world to make of it, but they knew well indeed that they better hurry or they might miss their homeward train.

THE ANOINTED

They met with the floor manager late in the afternoon as the sun went down behind the hills across the river and the light faded. The children quickly began fighting over the menu. Their mom insisted on having the fish casserole, but one of the daughters pointedly said, "Ma, you won't even be eating anything, so don't worry about it." Their Uncle Sydney showed up. He looked just the same as years before, the last time any of them had seen him since none of those kids like their cousins, Uncle Sydney's children from two marriages. The floor manager went over to the other side of the meeting room and said hello to Syd. She shook his hand heartily and noted that they hadn't seen each other for a few years at least. He replied that yes it had been a long time, too long and then he turned his attention to the other side of the room, agreed with his sister, and insisted on the fish casserole. The others wished their uncle hadn't arrived for the meeting. It's true, he might eat some casserole, but not his sister, no matter how much she insisted. At long last they all agreed on a menu and the floor manager left the room. Outside on the river one solitary ship framed by its string of deck-lights coasted downstream and out to sea.

HOUSE FOR SALE

The bed of old Wallace Stevens is less than you'd imagine: narrow, penitent, predictor of the grand conversion unproven. Here he added his own disorder to current disaster, ting-tang tossing through an ever-darkening night, demarcating lines into twos or threes as if that alone could provide some semblance of an order imagined if not actual. But here it is: the object itself that seems too short as well as too narrow to have ever contained such girth and height even if by then slackened with age and the despair that partners it. In the vacant and ordinary room there remains nothing of the occupant, not even this cot-like bed, not even a translucent ghost: one alone, warehoused some twenty miles south; the latter up late, up still, wandering in the nearby park, pacing off those lines, pacing forth the structure of ideas as the structure of things. Just how many rivers are there in this world? And how puny the number of names we know.

ONE AND TWO

I answer the part about how my generation could hear a guy do the real thing, guard down. I remember saying that the flag had started a plane for our saddest night. How long did the cousins sit around a table spending money, putting cynicism outside the window? I would disagree and deliver the goods to Connecticut. People said, "You seem like a nice guy." Then people in the church shouted and cursed, tossed the salad. Other times, I was handed an empty plate and a night crawler. And I'd never get out of town to the big room, but the thought of even less money created enough whispers to follow me. Nowadays I still feel it's the same. On the drive back whenever I go, wherever I go I end up wearing a pair of stilts like hearing a late winter crow trying to gather attraction. Well, it's the sleepless nights, I tell myself. I did some questioning at one point. I knew the evening and left a message. I made a little something extra. Why not? The porches and roofs had been a smudge on a window. I think it was in the morning as far away as the ocean. In another dream I would get to see the distance and stand-up in a market where I could hand-off the key, a good thing.

Second Generation

He moves some meat back and forth on his plate, meat removed from a bone. He looks at his wife and opens his mouth as if about to speak and not to eat, but before he can utter a word his wife, Julie, says, "It's a curse to be a good cook." Gian does not reply. He moves some more meat from a bone back and forth on his plate. Julie says, "This is good, Gian. This is legitimate barbecue. Don't you think so, Gian?" Julie pauses. "Yet," she sighs, "this is no different than what I would make at home. For us, Gian." She pauses again and looks right into the eyes of her spouse and says: "No one can surpass my lamb roast, Gian. No one." Then she lifts a wedge of meat above her plate, considers it a moment, and says, "But this is good. This is fine and legitimate barbecue. No Liquid Smoke. See that bark, Gian? That's from the rub they apply before placing the shank in their smoker. That's *legitimate* barbecue." Julie pauses for a moment, shifts in her seat and in her thought, and asks her husband of forty-years, "How did you like the estate sale?" And Gian looks at her for a moment and seems to consider his response, seems about to speak. Julie says, "I was disappointed. But I did want those swans. Didn't you? I thought about buying them as soon as we saw them. Remember the swans, Gian, the lovely swans? But then I saw that Not for Sale sign. And yes, I was disappointed. And you Gian? Were you disappointed?" And he says, "I didn't expect much." And then the waitress stops by to ask how everything is and if they would like anything else. Gian says he'd like to take his meat home and Julie adds, "And the chips, too." And then Julie reaches out for the forearm of the waitress, stops her from going, and says: "We were at an estate sale this morning—where we didn't buy anything even though we wanted the swans. And Gian said as we were leaving that he sure would like some barbecue. We were going to go elsewhere, somewhere known for their grilled burgers, that was the plan, but then Gian said he'd like some barbecue and I told him, I said, 'Gian, I read about a place not too far away' and so here we are and I want to tell you something, I want to tell you that this is legitimate. This is *legitimate* barbecue." The waitress smiles then — politely, professionally — and asks, "Would you like any desert?" "Oh, no," Julie replies. "I couldn't eat another thing." She turns away from the waitress, looks at Gian for some reason, and says, "When I first saw the sides I thought, 'these sides are too small.' But no, no. I was wrong: the sides and the cornbread along with the true and authentic barbecue. No, I couldn't eat another thing. I just couldn't. And you, Gian?" And Gian turns away from his wife and glances toward the waitress. "I'd like to bring this home," he repeats referring to what he left on his plate. "And the chips," Julie adds pointing to the basket. She would not leave empty-handed. "I'll wrap that right up for you," the waitress says with a competent smile. Julie moans, "I'm so full," leaning back in her seat and rubbing her stomach. "It's a curse," she says. "Yes, it is," Gian agrees as Julie sits up straight and wipes the remnants of lunch from her blouse.

INITIATIVE

Two of us did most of the talking and the other two were mostly silent. It was a small class. The university had proclaimed an internationalization of the curriculum but that apparently meant English only. Not so in our small unit of the university where English was never spoken. It felt good to stay on one's toes and listen intently less the train of thought be momentarily derailed, lost in this language that may be ancestral but is not native and remains for me somewhat foreign. As carefully as I listened, as cleverly as I replied I nonetheless had a feeling of guilt about the class, a feeling, so I imagined, that the two silent ones must share with me, even if for a different reason. For if they had left far too much during the weeks of the semester unspoken, I had left my bill unpaid. I did want to pay it. But this university does e-billing only and it must have gone, repeatedly, to the wrong email address. And when I emailed them to correct this error, I would receive an automated reply that the university no longer sends out bills via the post service and only uses e-billing. After several tries and nearly two-thirds of the semester I located a person who would respond to me. My obligation wasn't all I thought about during those weeks and, in fact, there must have been some days when I entirely forgot about the bill. I certainly gave much more thought to the class material then I did to the bill. When I reached that person in the Bursar's office, she agreed to forward my bill to me at the correct electronic address and in moments it appeared. I replied to this kind person that I would have a check off to the university in the next morning's mail. She had told me that my bill came to thirty-dollars. I am an employee of a nearby college and for a small registration fee we get to take courses at the university. I noted at the bottom of the bill which I printed so that I could send a check via surface mail that a late fee of one-dollar and fifty cents would be added. And so I wrote the check for thirty-one dollars and fifty cents, placed it in an envelope, and then in a US mailbox. In class the next morning I became unaccountably quiet and morose, which left poor Victor doing all the speaking, all the answering for the four of us. I excelled before I paid because there seemed to have been something clandestine and adventurous about that unpaid bill. Mild-mannered and unprovocative as I am, there was something taming and calming about having put the stamp on the envelope and then the envelope in the box, sending it off to an unnamed bank. My edge had been dulled; my enthusiasm, interest, and intensity lost. No sooner had this shift, this change been noticed than the semester ended, and with it any trace of the words we had spoken or those silences we would take with us into the next.

Rope Snake: A Fragment

Mid-state the children force everyday—sliding on windows. The cost, more insurance and investment slowing. We work together for a maximum high (the original window). They'll have to degrade Old Town mandates and our double hung garden, the mission our family takes to the governors. These rankings cross and tackle the best places; size cuts roughly the first redaction and while we pace our urge, we're also open to the plan. There's some relief, but still in conflict rooms always look better in lamplight in London at least. You can say "happy" and that would be enough. Our day of retreat lines up at the pavement's edge the blue and green standard lifted high and then returned, if not vanquished, hollowed out after the surrender. Dull sentinels of consumerism and consumption wave a flag of the nation ready for a battle.

There was something else: California. My grafting in with life took place in a small summer colony on the coast, chin in left hand and glad that no strand had escaped me. The book as funnel looked like everything narrowed to the present page or buried with saints or dogs. There the solitary uplift program, the concern for oranges, and always more leaves. He'd add oil and vinegar to memory and think, yes, poetry is business without money, too many cars. He had solid or sordid evidence. Was this more "truthful" than the *truth* one usually hears?

A wide range of stones huddled the avalanche that'd hook some relief, but still a conflict and an immigrant miner; a field trip to see it make a house stand up, to look at the man and take his pulse. Another person shakes their head, so eminent for piety— the saw that cuts the tree. A hand over the mouth and a few swept along or cemented, glued to the parlor. Oh and by the way, saved and strengthened were they and then pulled by two white horses.

Life in the West

It looks like Nixon is in the White House. I am lying in bed, in the lower berth of bunkbeds, listening to one song over and over again, dreaming about some wonderful point in the future, but not thinking about how to get there. Nixon is in the White House. My hands lift the machine, move it to the next room. It is black and white and boxlike. It looks like a rotary phone, a manual typewriter, or Nixon in the White House. I'll leave it on and hum a bit and spin round. "Fine work," and this I'll sing like Popeye the Sailor Man; alone and silent without a sea or an accomplice; off elsewhere and sorrowful.

A Thousand Words

Where the old dock stood, four pilings now and a walkway flat upon the water, flat and still and leading — this morning — to two small boats, secured and motionless, at rest, vacant — no one in sight, no sound, but quiet, quiet and still as darkest night but morning with morning light and nonetheless quiet, no one up and about, no one untying one little boat or the other, no one painting the old dock held up by those sturdy pilings, their message something like that of Stonehenge or maybe more like the Greek alphabet when seen from Oyster Bay.

Always the martial hymn. Many say oh that we might march on, march in our robes and hoods, holding high our flag. Here I am. Here I am, says the man with the thin tie. Those on the north side move against the parade; those on the south side follow it or stand still and watch it. All the men wear hats — white and black. All the women watching wear black and it seems thousands more march in white vestments crowned by white caps: war-nurses, still with hours of healing to provide.

If I were the girl in the picture I would have coaxed you to the vine (ignoring thorns) then coached you skyward — prosperous, luxurious. I would have restored the final vowel to our name and greeted you amidst a field of roses whose fragrance would have blinded our eyes for all the despair of loss within large families: one brother drops from the sky while others shake wherever they sit, land-bound. From white to black and white to a dark that offers no answers, I walk through the occasion merrily singing of what might be got out of the awaiting money bag.

With her sister she smiles. Her small hand rests on the ornate frill of her late century gown. Her left hand rests on sister's right shoulder. A carefully posed position for the photographer at the Stamford Portrait Studio, 170 State Street, date uncertain though back in the day when the abbreviation C-O-N-N meant Connecticut—no C-T as we use today—and back in the day when young women wore long, full dark dresses, the only frills allowed found in the ornate stitching. Their smiles, their smiles, as Cousin Peggy said after seeing the image …

With her husband everything appears to be very serious: the frivolities of childhood have been replaced by the necessities of parenthood, a few pounds gained in the giving birth to children and the worrying about them. How odd that their faces—husband and wife—over time have come to look so similar, a male and female version of the same person: same nose, same eyes, same full cheeks and high forehead. Yet he holds his right hand in a fist-like gesture and her left hides in a shadow behind her back. The backdrop itself: something out of the Hudson River School of painters, an imagined scene that year in Brooklyn.

He has returned unannounced but with time enough to pose singular and select in a series of rectangles: courtyard, window, and wall, hat slightly askew: at attention though surrounded only by walls, no island threats in the offing yet. And yet calculus required a set of nerves too if not quite the same ones as those required for the code breaking that's in the offing some months or a single year hence though far from the present zone of a mother's command. The window stays shut when depth of field turns toward death in the field.

It's funny. Whose leg? It must be Johnny's. Is it? (It's not so funny out on a Solomon island.) It's a wide, wide tie and a thin uplifted leg. No dirigible flew overhead through that day in Brooklyn. Then the war ended. Then the highway came and flattened the house. Looks like an old gun, looks like a flintlock that couldn't forestall the change that began when Iulio became Giulio and continued when Giulio became Julia. On an island someone waits out of sight for his return home to that house.

Her eyes in his direction yet there isn't a way to tell if she sees him, his back, or the sea, its coastline. Between them, her cousin, who lifts her glass of wine and drinks it, their table covered in white linen, the bottle half gone and only two chairs at present but had he some moments ago sat with them and told them of the new castle and the old and his own castle, *palazzo*, just a small castle, but grand enough, though its grandeur diminished some by Allied bombing? Now a time to rebuild. He leaves, cousin raises her glass, and she smiles pleased for the day and squints her eyes against its bright, bright sun.

One day before returning to New York, Professor Zoccoli gathered Nicola and Concettina and their daughter Anna Maria along with Concettina's brother Emilio for a picture. The Professor looks right at the camera. Nicola looks one way and Emilio the other way. Mother and daughter look in the same direction but Anna Maria's youthful eyes are a bit downcast while her mother's look forward as if she sees fast approaching the taxi or bus that'll take them to their next stop this day in Rome. Quick, Rebecca, snap the picture. And be sure to write on the back the names, the date, and the place of this mirage.

Yippee! At age forty one of you might be where you'd like to be — awake on the distant planet, afoot on its desert plane. And there a message from home: "season's greetings," simple but unsigned. In the lamplight the trees grow tall mid-ship providing figs and cantaloupe, sufficient to energize one expedition or another though never enough for a homeward flight through the red flames of a dying star.

In the field a highway
One parade into dark frills
A few eyes like that
Vowel sit fast hold on

LANDLOCKED

In my family we tell the tale that David Rizzio, consul and lover to Mary Queen of Scots, is our ancestor. Generation to generation we pass it on, and here I am perpetuating it in print. (This may not be rooted in historical fact.) I must say that at Holyrood Castle when the tour guide pointed out the spot were Rizzio fell from multiple knife wounds, I felt a thrill and wondered if the remnants of the DNA upon the floor might mirror my own. Yet, I remained silent and said nothing. If this heritage permitted me to vote perhaps I'd take the coward's way and abstain. Scotland is beautiful and I would vote for Edinburgh as the world's most beautiful city. Pride of place can be a good thing. But no land can exist without a currency, can it? One can barter with one's neighbor across a hedge, but not with one across an ocean. Borders perplex me. Cavour gave France Nice so the French would aid Italy's unification. Yugoslavia, gone; and Croatia got the coastline. And Northern Ireland and the Republic of Ireland: take out an old atlas, look at the map, and see if these divisions look like they make sense. And what about Long Island? Long Island should secede from New York and become part of Connecticut. Look at the map. 1915: Italy fancied Trieste and half a million Italians died.

MEMORIAL

The wood has recesses where once the body. The wood has
two shades one for the body. The mind had the will to outlive the
body: black squares against the white wind moored by the yellow
card of infraction, no ring-tone, no voice, no light—so many
squares. Midway a pyramid or diamond shape, the house of the
beneficiary, and the forest beyond, unaccounted for, unnamed.

AFTER AND BEFORE

The hollow of the cave, a black rock by its opening. No measure of sodium, a red band around the pole, a red cap atop. No flag blows in the wind. Rails run north south, a short distance. To the west, slats cordon an abyss. Grids of red and two shades of white lit by a light failing in the west. Beyond the hills out by the river a blue tower in the distance, a blue tower with a black band, designed with elegies, inscribed with paper days of bequest—redbird and yellow-pine; of protest—work-song and clock.

When I was young — back in the days of exponential suburban growth — door-to-door salesmen used to ring the front bell. This was the age of the Avon Lady, but also the cemetery man. Yes, he was thin, pallid and sallow. He could have used some blush. He offered Mom and Dad all sorts of combination packages but, alas, never made a sale.

When I was in high school, my summer job was mowing the lawn and trimming around the gravestones at the local Presbyterian cemetery, called Darlington. I used to joke to my friends who worked there with me, "Don't stop every time the Dead are on the radio." No grave digging for us — that was for union members, not high school students.

Now we've all grown older. I wondered recently if cemeteries, like neighborhoods, have sprawled to their limits. I had speculated that, for my generation, house prices would fall at the precise moment that funeral expenses rise. I wasn't thinking of the evangelical rapture when the tombs of the righteous shall be raised in clouds of glory, but of something simpler, dollars and cents; supply and demand. As the poet William Cullen Bryant put it, "All that tread / The globe are but a handful to the tribes / That slumber in its bosom."

One cemetery reports that only current or former residents who can establish their veteran status can pre-purchase. (Even having been the town's poet laureate, I'm told, won't help get me in those steely gates.) And then there is this odd sentence in the official description: "All other prior or current residents may purchase lots only on an immediate-need basis." At that moment, wouldn't the purchase be a bit late?

American cemeteries were prodigiously mocked in the British novelist Evelyn Waugh's 1948 novel *The Loved One*. This most solemn moment of life seems ripe for satire. One Connecticut cemetery claims it is the most picturesque in New England and that it offers views of Stamford harbor. Remember: this is a cemetery and not a new condo development. One Hartford cemetery pledges that "your final resting place will always be an integral and beautiful part of the overall landscape." Isn't "always" a rather difficult promise to make in such circumstances?

My sister tells me that there is room for more in my parents' plot. That makes sense to me since, while alive, they always had a spare room any of their kids could occupy when needed. As I said, they didn't purchase "eternal slumber" space from that door-to-door salesman. How they came to these graves, like so much else regarding final things, is a bit of a mystery. One thing bothers me about this particular shady grove. Theirs is right by a Paramus, New Jersey golf course with frequent cart traffic on the other side of a tall hedge. An errant drive could break the contemplative mood and crack your noggin.

My wife tells me that her parents, still alive, unlike mine, also have purchased a plot with extra spaces. But theirs is a Jewish cemetery, and though I have an ecumenical spirit, I cannot convert. Plus, this cemetery sprawls near the intersection of the New Jersey Turnpike and the Garden State Parkway. Unlike the Stamford one, there seems to be little that is picturesque here.

Pine Grove Cemetery in Waterbury solved the problem of overcrowding by dividing and expanding. There are now two Pine Groves: Old and New. Much to my surprise, one of the state's most historic cemeteries — Grove Street Cemetery in New Haven — encircled by a formidable fence and hence of limited growth potential, has room for more burials.

There's Cedar Hill Cemetery, nearby in Hartford, final resting place for many of the region's famous: industrialists, politicians, performers, and, yes, poets. There's a memory for me here already. Once, about a decade ago, I won a four-mile race in this park-like cemetery.

I better hurry now, get running to take care of this plot problem in life's narrative before the price of the most simplistic sepulcher tilts skyward. Henry Wadsworth Longfellow claimed, "There is no Death! What seems so is transition; / This life of mortal breath / Is but a suburb of the life elysian, / Whose portal we call Death." To be continued? Perhaps.

Pass Go and Collect

One sunny afternoon in May after finishing a brief hike in a state park I fell over next to my car in the parking lot. Someone called for an ambulance and I went to the nearest hospital where they discovered they had to open me immediately and replace this with that and sew me up and send me on my way. That had been quite a blow, a derailment that knocked me from my tracks for five or six months and yet the events of a different day a little more than one year later devastated me.

The day he died I had been out mowing the lawn enjoying the sun beating down on me, something I refrained from doing the summer before—doctors' orders. I showered after, put on some clean clothes, went downstairs and poured a glass of white wine, went back upstairs, turned on the computer, performed the necessary preliminaries, and looked at the list of messages. There to my surprise was one from a name recognized but unfamiliar with a subject line that included a name both recognized and familiar, a name for several decades bibliographically at least closely associated with mine own or maybe I should reverse that order and say mine with it, but nonetheless the subject line importuned bad news, sad news, final news, or in short, the end.

When I fell in that state park parking lot I felt no pain and little discomfort. For much of that troubling time it had been as if my body separated from my mind and the latter looked down upon the former with distant and cold clinical interest.

Electronic mail. For someone who grew up when we did and can hear the sound of the old truck a mile distant or the step a block away, such a term seems an affront or an oxymoron at best. *Electronic mail.* One believed for decades that the phone could ring at some odd hour and if it did the news would be of a parent's demise or something far worse, a nephew's or a niece's. But electronic mail—there it is with no dreaded ring, no mile distant engine ... there it is amidst returned films received, requests for advice on historic homes ... there it is — passed away.

And when did this euphemism become so popular? Everyone now says "passed away." In the class the student says last year my grandpa passed. At the dinner party the nice real estate lady says a year ago my husband passed. Pass go and collect two-hundred dollars. Why don't they just say died, dead, and kaput?

Let's not be crass, but my second or third thought was this: where does this leave me? When a parent or child dies that is one thing but when the voice of your generation and for your identity *passes* that is something else entirely. If one makes you angry and open to impossible deals such as take me first God please the other sets you adrift on a sea of despondency. Now what?

No more the expectation of a new book outside the door, retrieving it, and sitting with it through an entire day reading each new page from cover to cover non-stop. But all that has gone before remains for the perusal of graduate students in search of an acceptable dissertation topic and so the correspondence will arrive from Geneva and Tokyo; Palermo and Prague. More explanations of the bent genres and strong but indecisive characters offered for inspection and advice but most of all for encouragement — never say a discouraging word. What would be the purpose?

There before me in the clearest phrase possible appeared disheartening words final words addressed to a list of one-hundred names, those same names that would receive the latest book at their door always accompanied by the cryptic card noting in bold type "gift of the author" without any name or conversely with a name — that of the publisher — and no words of greeting such as "gift of the author." All the names for the message had been disclosed, perhaps mistakenly. There were all the ones I expected, some that I did not recognize, and a few that quite frankly surprised me such as the chauvinistic old professor from Yale. (Our author attended Princeton and not Yale and did not share, I am sure of it, the old professor's views.) You see, I had studied that list closely, even before reading the message completely.

What had I hoped to find therein? My own sense of inclusion in the contemporary world of letters, I suppose, or some inkling that here I am amidst the living and not yet joining hands with the dead — if that's anything like what the dead do after dying. I don't know. But at just the moment I completed the message proper I heard a ferocious growl from the pit of my gut and I clicked off the message but left the laptop on. After I had something to eat, then I would respond, then I would send my condolences and sincerest regrets and ask if there is anything I can do.

No sooner had I returned from downstairs, however, then a second message for the committee of one-hundred awaited our attention informing all of the details of the service. It seems that at the end tradition would be upheld and burial would be almost immediate. It seemed, therefore, all I could do would be to alter, slightly, my plans for the next few days and attend.

Let me begin at the beginning. I once had a friend — an elder friend, a mentor of sorts — who constantly mailed me paperback books he had worked on one way or another for one large publisher or another. I read some of them but certainly not all of them for at that time I had to keep up with the rigors of graduate school course syllabi. But one book in particular caught my attention. I'm not sure why it did so before I had even read a sentence of it. If I remember right there had been no special cover design, no spiffy title, and no famous name above or below the title. Yet when I read the first sentence, when I by chance opened that book and read that sentence and not any other one I knew immediately — though at the time I would have been unable to articulate this knowledge to myself — that I would have to read every other sentence not only in the volume I held in my hand but every other one that this author would create. The sentence, then, I knew it at the start — these sentences fit the reader's mind like a glove, a mixed-metaphor I suppose, but there you have it: words for both the body and the mind which together yes do indeed elevate the soul. Sentences so bound together that to read them one enters a state of reverie.

I had been blessed by the gift that morning of this cheap paperback reprint of the author's obscure first book. And so it began.

I wrote a short piece immense in its praise of the book for the local paper. And then one day perhaps three weeks later a postcard arrived in nearly illegible scrawl from the author himself thanking me for the praise that he said quite frankly embarrassed him in its profusion, but, he added, the theme that I had identified (though I almost buried any analysis in the praise) he thought plausible. "I'm glad you pointed that out," he said and promised to send a copy of his next book due out "imminently."

As things often do in publishing that second book took longer than its author hoped or thought. Though an artist always, he did keep an eye out for his own bottom line and calculated that the paperback edition of his first book might give his second book a little boost and vice-versa, time was key. But it took the publisher six months at least and maybe ten though certainly not an entire year to get it out. And so when a taped and bound with string, slightly damaged envelope addressed by the author himself in his barely legible hand arrived at my door I had all but forgotten about the promised gift though I had not by any means forgotten about the author. Indeed, I continued to praise that first book and even bought ten copies to give to my brother, my sister, one much admired professor, and some of my local writing friends.

Over the ensuing thirty year period we met face to face only three times I think and certainly not more than a half-dozen times. We wrote to each other occasionally and exchanged books. (I'm certain I got the better end of this deal. Mine to him remained always in hand-printed make-shift envelopes without any ambiguous publisher's card.) It must have been around the time of his third novel that we met for the first time at a diner not too far from his house and now we meet one last time at a memorial park not too distant in space even if it is in time from that diner, Lucky's Diner. The refrain I suppose would have to be *what have you got to lose*? Let's see. Can we make a list: a friend, a moral compass, a voice grander than Caruso and Sinatra combined, a giver of gifts that came to my door with compliments of the author? What does that mean? It is too late to ask. Can I ask the family? Definitely not. Can I ask the publisher? Yes, but some years ago our mutual friend—also a writer—once warned us, don't believe a thing a publisher tells you.

I didn't know who to talk to when I arrived at the event. I offered my condolences to the wife and children. A couple of graduate students who had met with me over the past few years were there and yet I felt out-of-place with the many celebrities from the world of high society literature or that of music and film. There seemed no space reserved for the adventuresome authors of Small Press Distribution best-sellers. To my chagrin I ended up next to his publisher.

She greeted me warmly. Why wouldn't she. After all, for several decades I had done something to keep her top-selling author selling to an audience of intellectual refinement—the university world of readers in other words: that would be intelligentsia. Though I thought of my work as scholarly or at least as literary criticism I think she regarded me as a valued member of their marketing department. I suppose there may be some truth to that though whatever I accomplished amounted to far less than glowing reviews in global dailies or seemingly off-hand endorsements from the world's most famous film directors. She held out her hand to me and I gently shook it. We looked at each other and saw that we both had tears in our eyes (it was a funeral after all) and then she offered me the seat next to hers and there I sat.

She also offered a book deal of my own, not for something of mine *per se*, but a quickly cobbled together overview of our deceased friend's life and work. In between the Rabbi's prayer and the Pulitzer-Prize winner's eulogy, she would sketch out some of her thoughts for me. I hesitated, but felt curiously disloyal for having done so and also rationalized that such a publication might help sell a few copies of my unsellable tomes. And so I said yes. I agreed to turn out something part memoir, part biography, and part appreciative interpretation all within two months' time which I thought might mean some well-chosen photos included but no poetry allowed.

And so I returned to Litchfield ready to begin. I thought I would describe the funeral service. It remained fresh in my mind and so many of the people in his life attended that simple recall and description would make for a readable, though sad, and meaningful opening. But, I conjectured, he wrote more of life than death, though I wouldn't go so far as to say more of love than death. Eros and Thanatos—the two big themes. What else is there to talk about? Once the marching orders are written it is easy to follow with a much longer double-file: war and peace, rich and poor, old and young, city and country and so on.

Every reader knows the bare bone facts of his life and all literate folks know some of his work. What had I agreed to—a publisher's ploy to turn a quick dollar after an unexpected death or my own desire to write something easy, not out of necessity, to assuage a damaged ego more than a shallow pocket? I had enough income, a steady position that provided time enough to turn out a book of some sort every two years or so and income sufficient enough to render the question of sales of that work one of interpretation, of disdain, of self-justification and certainly not one of appeal or need.

Even now did I still want to be so dependent on the deceased, so posthumously linked? To write of an author one decade my senior would be difficult—like if I were to write of my sister of the same age. What do I know of anyone born in that year? Far easier it would be to write of the long ago deceased parent.

What have I gotten myself into? I wondered as I walked down the street to the Village Restaurant where I planned to sit by myself with a beer, slowly nursed, and figure this out, but Dan, the bartender, decided that I would be the object of his interest, his inquiries, and conversation this fine afternoon.

"Why so glum?" he asked. I hadn't realized I looked particularly glum or any other recognizable way.

I replied, "I just got back from a funeral."

"That's tough," Dan said.

"Not so tough for me. Tougher for him," I wittily added.

"Maybe," he said. "Sometimes it's harder on the living."

I nodded. He paused and then asked, "Friend or relative?"

"Friend," and then I paused. "Well, more a colleague of a sort then a friend, I guess."

"You don't sound very sure of yourself."

"I'm not. Believe me, I'm not."

He wiped the bar-top and I continued, speculatively, "We grew up in the same state, but in different towns and a decade apart—which makes a big difference when you're young; less so as you get older."

"That's correct," Dan agreed.

"Had we been the same age and had we attended the same schools, I think we would have been members of different cliques, though certainly with some overlap."

"Okay. So you weren't a relative of the deceased and you weren't a friend but a 'colleague' from the same state but still a different time, place, and, so it sounds, sensibility. Why'd you attend his final rites then?"

"He was a writer, very well-known, and I wrote about him from the book that launched his fame until—so it seems—after his burial."

Dan looked at me askew. "That's cryptic," he said. "A bad pun, I know, but what do you mean?"

And so I told him how I felt obligated to go to his funeral and by chance I sat next to his publisher and she asked me to turn out a quick tribute book in his memory.

"And that makes you sit here with a beer looking glum? That doesn't sound like a bad assignment—colleague or friend, friend or colleague. Get started," he chided me.

"It's not so simple," I moaned.

Dan was right: it needn't be complex. Either I sat down and did it or I didn't. My choice. I knew enough—backwards and forwards. And the pay I had been offered to churn this out seemed significant. In fact, more than I had ever been offered for any sort of writing project.

At home I checked for messages first off and there near the top I saw that I had one from Hillary, probably the very top student I had ever taught. Her message thanked me for several books I had given her, ones I didn't need to keep and ones authored by friends who taught at a couple of the universities she had been thinking about for graduate school. And she said, "Thank you for helping me become a better writer. I will never forget all you've done for me."

Those two sentences made so much worthwhile — the anti-intellectualism of contemporary higher education; the administrative bloat — gluttony might be more accurate, had been so discouraging lately. "The justification for universities is not to certify that there are so many course units per square head, but to advance knowledge and to teach it. We should do what we came to do, and to hell with the administration." Unfortunately things have decayed a lot since Murray G. Murphey penned those lines several decades ago. Now, alas, the esteemed administrators can't even count heads.

Hillary had written two long works of fiction her senior year, both of them in that no man's land (like some of her professor's work) of a novella's length, though one moves in continuous narration and the other jumps about in brief chapters. What most moved me were her enthusiasm for the tasks, that old abstraction *imagination* that she brought to bear upon those tasks, and most of all the language employed to do so. To borrow a phrase from the poet Wallace Stevens, hers is a prose that wears the poem's guise, hers is a supreme fiction or, at least, one in embryo, one about to be born.

As I sat there in front of that screen that stared back at me almost in accusation I wondered if it might be better for someone young and quite frankly brilliant to take on the contract project, someone new, rather than another writer who knew him from the start. I toyed with the idea of hitting reply to message and asking if Hillary might be interested in a bit of ghost writing.

Here's how I had it figured. I did not feel like the labor of it, but the benefits in terms of prestige did interest me. While the money offered had been generous for me it could not make much of a difference in the larger scheme of things. I have a decent job with an okay salary. What really might matter or so I thought would be the advertisement for myself that such a publication would produce. Then there was the fact that Hillary had been offered tuition at a few of the schools, but not a single stipend for living arrangements. Quite frankly, this angered me a little. I knew she'd be as good as or better than other students in her grad program, but since she graduated from a small, indistinct institution prejudice and condescension would greet her every step of her way. And so she who so loved writing in and of and for itself, she who had a genius of language could ghost write the thing. She'd get the money; I'd get the spin. She had some familiarity with the books in question for she had read some of them in classes I taught and others on her own. I'd be around or at least just an email address away to answer any questions that might come up and I could provide a few anecdotes to give the thing that proper true to life human tone.

Or maybe I should take on a co-writer and be more upfront about the whole thing. Or maybe I should call and back out. So I wondered. How did I get myself into this? Or maybe the prayers should have been for me. Maybe, if our places had been altered, he could have been talked into delivering the eulogy. A far-fetched thought perhaps, but who knows? And maybe that eulogy might have been just the ticket. Maybe my books might have witnessed a sudden uptick in sales during the days and nights that followed their author's demise.

A Moral Fable

Once upon a time there was a professor who lived by the sea. One day he went fishing and caught three fish.

The professor went fishing the next day, and he caught nothing.

His friend took him fishing on a boat. They did not catch any fish.

His friend said, "I am sorry. We have been struck with misfortune."

The professor replied to his friend: "No. No, we should be content. I always say — enjoy what you get."

"Yes. Yes," his friend started to say. "But we haven't got ... "

The professor interrupted. "No 'but.' Please, let us go to a tavern. And there we will drink white wine."

And so they went.

ICARUS

I remember the way the dry wood felt in my hands. It had the feel of the branch of a tree more than some man-made thing. I didn't need the job. Someone thought it would be good for me, teach me the value of a dollar. In the greenhouses were thousands of empty pots and my job was to put a bulb in a pot, then fill it with fertilizer and dirt, pat the mixture down, move on, and so on. The owner said I planted the bulbs all wrong. He tried to show me the right way to do so but I couldn't see how what he did differed from what I had done and I told him so and that might have been my mistake. I can remember how the shovel felt full of soil that steamed early in the morning and dried out, lightened as the day wore on and the sun rose in the sky heating everything.

AMSTERDAM

What could I have written in the application to garner their attention? No matter what, it sufficed. And in the dark of an early February (or was it mid-month?) we flew in the darkness of that year to Amsterdam.

We had been there once before on vacation: seven or eight days during which we stayed in a small hotel near the Anne Frank House. This second trip we were to stay for more than five months and in a grand house on the Keizersgracht not far from the Leidseplein.

Two or three boxes of books, perhaps four, had been shipped in advance. At the airport we waited with huge backpacks stuffed full as if to embark on an expedition. From Schiphol into the Center we took a taxi since our heavy packs weighted us so. The driver sped along the short distance at a speed approaching that of our airplane. When we landed at the massive front steps of our residence the sun had just about risen as much as it would during that dark northern month. We felt tired from the trip, but jubilant for the arrival. Our hosts and landlords, the Zellers, greeted us. We had rented the larger of their two top floor apartments. Our neighbor, up high above the Keizer's canal, we would see only occasionally and fleetingly. He travelled a lot for work and rarely came home and then, only for brief periods of rest before he'd be off again to Venice or Heidelberg.

Our apartment overlooked the canal and had a sleeping alcove, a large living room, a dining area, a small kitchen, a study, and a bathroom.

This was a time in my life when I felt there might be too many expectations placed on me as an American or a husband or a poet. I might have to represent my country in this one. I might have to leave the room early to return to our temporary home high above the canal at Keisergracht 419. I might have to answer some questions about a poet like Anthony Hecht who attended the same college as I did and whose work I had read in graduate school, but I didn't like it then and had forgotten it by the time of my lecture in Brussels.

This was a time in my life when I didn't want to be singled out as an artist but wanted to receive credit and praise for all and any work created and so when we broke into groups of seven at Terschelling to co-author poems — the leaders' idea of an icebreaker — I didn't want to take charge of our group or have any responsibility for it, for what we produced, and yet nonetheless I suggested a casually produced cut-up so that we might continue our chatting and gossiping though I feared the group led by a physicist would out write us as indeed they did for they created a perfect sonnet of both substance and song while we offered but a puzzle of abrupt shifts that didn't even lead to a smile or a snicker.

And this was a time in my life when it could be difficult to negotiate life with two of us involved in it. Like at the tavern later that night when I wanted to stay longer and hang out with the graduate students but you wanted to go back to our room after the very first beer and did not want to stay and insisted that I go in every way possible without actually saying so.

Yet there had been no need for concern. The poem got published in England; the lecture, presented in Belgium. The latter led to applause followed by an invitation for return. And as for leaving the tavern early that night: because we turned in early we got up and out early and there in the dunes we saw the terns on the sand and the ospreys above and all was well, wonderful, and together as it had never been before.

Literature, friends, walking, and going places: the plan. On the walls were rural scenes: a barn, a cow, a haystack. I wanted to ask for one to bring home, but we had just arrived.

And no sooner had we arrived then the consulate sent a car to take us to the ambassador's reception in Den Hague. I had heard that Gore Vidal would be there and I assumed he would be eager to meet me, a younger writer who would carry forward a great tradition and not pander to prurient interests or cheap sentimentalism, but upon our arrival he seemed locked into an over-stuffed chair and hesitated to rise, to shake one's hand.

And so after a polite visit for the required time we left with one of the Dutch professors and searched for a Chinese restaurant which we found with little difficulty and while I cannot recall the quality of the food I do remember that we could not find a taxi after and our host and his wife argued a bit about how we would reach the train station in time for the last train.

We did, though. And then we rested briefly, and then we flew to London where we saw our nephew before taking a train to Southampton where I lectured to attentive graduate students. Denise went back to the room while I joined the class at a pub. I further defined for the students what I meant by the Postmodern canoe while Denise ordered out for Chinese food. When I returned she seemed unhappy that I had been away for so long or, as I tried to explain, so brief a time. It is a matter of perspective, I offered.

I brushed my teeth and then climbed into bed, but an incessant tapping kept us awake half the night. It turned out that our hostelry took pets and the noise through the night had been nothing more than the repetitive tap of a retriever's tale. Perhaps the dog had better dreams than ours. And we rose early in the morning to start for Stonehenge.

Back in Amsterdam three days later we listened to Dan Jacobson read his "sticky bread" story and then stopped at a Chinese restaurant on the Kerkstraat just off the Leidseplein. We walked home and upon entering I realized I had left the Nikon at the restaurant, slung over the back of my chair, no doubt. And so we went back out, returned to the restaurant, and retrieved the camera. There it was just as I thought it would be slung to the back of a chair, but still I was incredulous. When we got back home—to stay this time—I couldn't get over it. I had forgotten the Nikon!

Yet, it is true that a camera was not necessary. Weeks, months, or years later I'd be able to recall and recount with remarkable precision where we were on a particular day and what we did on it, who we saw, what we ate, the time of sunrise, and the color of the sky at sunset. There was the day of the seminar for teachers in a small room at the national library in Brussels and after I spoke to them and before our lunch had been served, I sat at the table with folded hands and one teacher conjectured that I desired to offer grace before the meal. And once in Luxembourg City the kind professor said, yes, he knew Pierre, but more particularly Pierre's father. And on a boat one day a jovial middle-aged woman praised Dutch ingenuity with enthusiasm bordering on excess. Who could have known then that one day it would be too painful to remember anything of those months after too many years had elapsed, after pens had lost their green ink; people, their lives?

On Monday May thirteenth an ambulance rushed me from the parking lot at Penwood State Park to the emergency room of the closest hospital. On the way I received an injection of Atropine and chewed some children's aspirin. At the time my pulse rate had dropped to the low-thirties.

I waited — prostrate — in a small room in the emergency wing from mid-afternoon to mid-evening. Denise waited with me and our nephew Mark, a PA at the hospital, waited with us. During this time an emergency room nurse and doctor monitored my condition. Around 9:30 p.m., I moved to a single room that would be my home for several nights.

The next day a cardiologist and neurologist examined me. They thought I had a TIA or near-stroke. That afternoon an echo-cardiogram revealed a heart anomaly. This led to further tests and to careful consideration of any relation between the TIA and the heart defect. Would it be safe to operate should I require surgery?

The next day, my third in the hospital, a trans-esophageal exam revealed at least one tumor on my aortic valve. A surgeon now became part of my medical team. Yet, there remained the question of timing and safety of any surgical procedure. Late that night I had a MRI scan to help answer this question and to see the nature of the damage caused by the near-stroke.

The following day I had three CT scans and an additional MRI. These tests showed that I had a small stroke in a minor artery on the left side of my neck (a spontaneous dissection) and that the stroke had not been caused by a free-floating piece of the tumor.

The surgeon and others — after consultation with staff elsewhere — decided I needed immediate surgery because of leakage from the aortic valve. Friday morning from seven to eleven, the open heart surgery team operated on me. The surgeon discovered in addition to the tumor, two calcifications. He replaced my aortic valve, which he later described to the cardiologist as "ugly, ugly."

After surgery, I woke up in a noisy recovery room where I spent the night. The next day I moved to "8-9," a cardiac care floor and stayed there Saturday afternoon through Monday afternoon. Then I returned home.

Before surgery I felt invincible and now I feel vulnerable. Now liberty exists only in a library and that library has been shipped to New Jersey.

Donald went to the professor and asked for an extension and the professor replied that he could not do so and that if he made an exception for Donald he'd have to make an exception for everyone. Now that wouldn't be right, would it? But only Donald had asked for an extension.

The panel organizers had arranged for a car service to take three of us from Schiphol into the city. The drive to the Adams Institute I knew would be short but my wait at the airport was long. Our flights were staggered and I landed first. The flight from Logan had been uneventful and I longed to return to the city, but first there would be the wait for my two colleagues. As if some hierarchy governed the duration of this pause, we whisked off in our car once the third and most famous member of our merry trio arrived from Newark.

Harry huffed and puffed the whole way while Tom anxiously fidgeted and I tried to mediate, placate, and calm. Perhaps it was the long flight followed by the long wait but for a second I dosed off and during that moment of rest brought on by exhaustion I dreamed that I had become a goose flying somewhere above the polders of the Netherlands. My flight had something frantic about it for the other members of the flock were nowhere to be seen and yet a loud honking noise came from the sky just in front of me and I flapped hard as goose-possible hoping to catch up to my bird friends and family. Then, behind me far in the distance, I heard a plane's engine and its ever-increasing roar. Then I became a passenger on that plane with a window seat and I looked upon a flock of geese falling from the sky, shredded by a jet engine's rotors. The plane seemed to stutter or leap for a second and then the loud belch of Harry woke me once more to the present and our land bound approach to Amsterdam.

It seems that in those moments of my brief repose Harry and Tom had commenced a conversation or perhaps a debate regarding the relative merits or lack thereof of literary awards and prizes. It surprised me to hear the vehemence in which Harry lashed out against them but my reaction may have been predicated upon the fact that he spoke so loudly not yet fully understanding the ramifications of his recent partial loss of hearing.

"CALVINO," Harry shouted. "CALVINO. Now there's a man of principle. Wins the Strega Prize. Refuses it. Moves to France."

"But then the Italians hated him," Tom added.

And I asked, "Would either of you refuse such an accolade?"

Tom ignored me. Harry repeated, "Accolade."

"And Mulisch," Tom began. "He practically nominated himself for the Nobel. All that barely masked pleading in *The Procedure*."

A misreading, I thought. Mulisch meant that it is better to be alive and have no prize than to be dead and in a grave with the big award alongside.

"Well, he never got it," Harry interrupted.

And I offered, "He died too soon."

"Perhaps," Harry said somewhat sardonically.

I looked at him with I think completely unmasked disbelief and noted, "Mulisch is my favorite author."

Harry interrupted with one word, "Sycophant. And if we were in France tonight would you choose Robbe-Grillet?"

And Tom wondered, "And what about our guest of honor? That's why we're here," he added. "To celebrate the living and not the dead."

"And Ralph Waldo Emerson and Charles Brockden Brown," I continued.

Tom asked if all my favorite authors have three names and I said no, Mulisch was just Harry. Harry Mulisch.

And Tom stretched out his legs. "Ah, Harry. Like our friend Harry. Here with us now. Harry, how are you?"

"Fine, Tom. Fine."

And the car slowed down by the Adams Institute, named for the second president of the United States and the first US ambassador to the Netherlands.

"Gentlemen. We have arrived," our driver reported after parking in a reserved spot out front.

We tumbled out like schoolboys. Perhaps the three of us were eager to see our friend, the guest of honor, and eager to speak, too. We entered the gracious and grand room. The fourth member of our roster, the star of our team sat alone on the stage across the packed hall. We had arrived fifteen-minutes or so late, fashionably late. We walked briskly through the low-lit space, took our seats, and mumbled some low-voiced greetings and apologies. We were ready to begin.

SECOND THOUGHTS

It has become easy to speak to an audience after more than forty years of doing so. Nonetheless, I rely on my lessons from seminary still. I use three examples: always, it seems, three. I end invariably with a charge to my audience. I begin by setting out the scope and purpose of what I'll say. I consider the composition of my audience and adapt my words accordingly. I speak slowly always and rarely from notes, slowly because I have no notes and slowly because an audience may not be familiar with what I say, with all that I've learned during these decades or think I have learned. I recalled today that I had spoken here at this site some thirty-five years ago. On my first visit I spoke much faster. Then I may have had a prepared text too. (It is hard to remember.) Then I assumed of my auditors a certain level of knowledge, third year seminary at least! The challenges we face today are so onerous I warned at the close of my second appearance. My time is so brief: fifty minutes. My time in the midst of everything grows short. I don't know how much I have left and no watch will suffice. I pray that I can impress upon all the seriousness of these matters without revealing my growing skepticism of any God's benevolent plan. And that I now doubt the efficacy of prayer.

SLOW ROASTED

They were with us for almost a year. Their work was precise and perfect, but so slow. They stained the cabinets by hand on wooden horses in the living room. They knocked down and re-built three walls; replaced them in new configurations. And when they finished we had fun showing visitors how the drawers closed slowly on their own, how the wood had a picturesque grain, how the granite fit the scheme. But after they packed their tools and we paid the bill, the time had arrived for a trial run; that is, to cook something. And so we decided to make a pizza pie. We had made the dough early that morning using standard ingredients of water, yeast, and brown sugar; and flour, olive oil, salt, plus some more water. I like the way the yeast smells, but that stout odor gets lost as soon as the liquid mixes with the flour, oil, and salt. I do not like mixing and pounding the dough and the way some of it seems to stick to skin for a day or two after no matter how vigor-ous one's hand washing, no matter how hot and soapy the water. We let the dough rise in our new oven throughout the day, took it out, and pounded it down when ready for use. We broke up some broccoli, sliced some plum tomatoes, added chopped black olives, and sprinkled cheese and oregano on top. The least ingredient—oregano—produced the strongest smell as our pizza cooked. And here's the way it all worked out. Our perfect kitchen produced a perfect pizza. The peppers had a delicious crisp taste. But wait a second. What peppers? It was broccoli and olives. And so ours had become a magic kitchen—a transformative kitchen as well as one transformed.

SOMETHING BORROWED

We planned to eat dinner at the Royal Buffet, but first in a paradox that is central to the logic of emotional texture, our historians measured the significance of a typical storm. By contrast, the legitimacy of so-called natural identities erased an era from the idiotic and then the sustenance of public meals. In an editorial published in suburban areas, a pampered Maud eventually subjected signs to her immediate home, an old but impoverished estate. She could think of the farther hills, the village contained in an irresolvable narrative. Unlike the connection between success and power, she colored her house's structure to give her interests an authentic identity and the consolation of many satisfying catalogs. She may have lost a decorator's call when the department stores generated some few sentimental customers. The lesson expressed comes with experience. Elsewhere our sociologists regulated the community and what some meant when darkness everywhere became a new house that would probably never become the antithesis of particular sacrifices and uneasiness. Home may indicate contradictory identifications. Boundaries increase into general use the promises of authority not to eschew the answer. Homeownership when managed as well as the erosion of a book-length study has been marked by the demand and the best-known manufactures. Those who could not conceal their disgust twist in meaningless limitations and have historically undergone the hostility which others examine on the periphery of our city. Yet those who are the most subsidized see domination rather than the dream. There has been no destination and forward stopped being a direction long ago.

FATIGUE IS SCRAWNY

Several factors may contribute to the development of fast-growing pockets of hostile psychological needs, the implications of a location not specified. In contrast to categories simultaneously spatial and functional, some walk downtown using an essentially new mode of redress. In fact, development of mixed-use stores and perfectly predictable destinations result in one of our most stunning concepts. Although I think the by-now-familiar terms and patterns are reasons no one will describe the role of the pseudonym. Of course, we aren't all mixed in front porches, cul-de-sac streets, and outdoor activities. A picture emerges as one factor wedges into existing homes. But another point of view, I suppose, is whether there appears to be some backlash in the lines required for gas stations and railroad tracks down by a double-occupancy room? With regard to the outcomes talked about in a two-tier market, we are now reaching a special, magical edifice called the Crystal Pavilion. What I noticed was the pressure that arose in showing us the need for the new. Certainly I am not enthusiastic as I think back to the often described Sputnik. A second area became transparency and the word *fundamental* required a focus on people who use bicycles instead. What is obvious to many is quoted. Although the plan outlines the failure of that concept, I do not believe any impact of the controversy surrounding a scene of isolation in these areas provides conventional partitions. Furthermore, the transparency we are talking about, the emphasis in this relationship forces members of our culture toward excellence. In an odd way the relationship between long hours subjected to public transportation and the stresses people feel have an advantage for at least some portion of our interactions and that fact carries with it the urge to reduce variations in the number of extremes related to what is called a neighborhood. Thus we have arguably addressed balance and the total number to be addressed. Repeatedly we question the evolution of integrated cities where the supermarket changes the way people take the event known as a *display* to another expansion of the "yes." Speaking about the use of location, one of course asks, why can't goods have as many motives as consumers? Teenagers essentially parallel experience. And so over the years, comments about this problem invariably contrast shopping and words. We shall see. Although there remains at least one place where the process if not the terminology of the idea of development exists in the psychology of these spaces, these messages, it is not necessarily both hard to ignore and known as the best we have. Alas, when I began this vision: how vast its future!

HER THIRTEENTH LETTER

This is not the first attempt and it will not be the last. The box of tissues has half its contents still. How to get said what she wants to say? Precisely. The red of the table and blue of the wall offer little to stir or calm her mind. She leans forward and away from the stiff slats of the chair in which she sits. She could have chosen the upholstered chair. She could have chosen to stand by the window and wait. And still she writes; the curtain open and the table cloth a brilliant though mottled red; her hands almost claws by now as they reach back to the start to tell it all over again once more.

MIRACLE

Yeshia lived to be one-hundred and when he died the family cut up his clothing and distributed the pieces. People believed that having a bit of clothing worn by a man who had lived so long would bring good fortune and long life. People forget that though Yeshia had long life he rarely had good fortune.

Yeshia used to say that if he were a millionaire he'd fill his pockets with raisins. Although he worked hard, he made only a meagre living and would have most likely starved had it not been for the abundant fish from the nearby river.

Yeshia had a single child, Leah, a sweet, pretty girl whose mother had died soon after giving birth. Yeshia and Leah planted pumpkin vines around their small plot of land. Leah learned how to make pumpkin bread and pumpkin soup. Each morning when her father left to work in the fields, she would tend the pumpkins. Before hoeing the soil she spat on the ground three times to ward off bad luck.

It seemed to work, too, for all went smoothly for some time — time enough so that they almost forgot all of life's problems. But then when least expected, an unwanted notice arrived followed a week later by a small escort of soldiers charged with bringing Yeshia and other men of the village to the city and then from there — no one knew where.

Leah cried and cried. She soon ate the last of the pumpkin bread and soup. She soon ran out of sunflower seeds. She became despondent and then ill. One of the ancient women of the village gave her a flask of golden medicine and instructions on how and when to take it.

One night a message arrived, brought by a handsome young man who soon disappeared into the night. Yeshia had escaped. He sent many krona and a map. On it he had placed an X and had written a time and a date and nothing more.

Leah had never been outside the bounds of her village beyond which the tall trees of the forest grew skyward rendering the land dark, dark and dangerous for she had heard the tales of evil spirits and bandits.

In the cover of darkness the next night she said goodbye to her pumpkin patch and began her long trek. As she walked she felt better, stronger. She did not know if it were because of her exertion or because of the medication in the flask. After a fortnight she reached the outskirts of the city. She could see the lights of the steelworks from atop the hills.

When she reached the prescribed address on Willow Street there was Yeshia, open-armed and ecstatic, but looking older, a bit worn and gray. They hugged as if they would stay entwined that way for all of history.

But eventually Yeshia spoke. First, he thanked God. Then he complimented his brave daughter. And then he thanked his young friend Velvil who had risked his life to get the map and krona to Leah. Yeshia told Leah that their struggles had not ended. The city would be, for them, but a meeting place and soon nothing more than a memory. Their destination had been decided for them. Relatives had settled in New Britain, Connecticut and this American place would be their goal, their destination and future home.

They walked and they rode and they sailed. Then they boarded a train and at the small station distant cousins who spoke their language greeted them, embraced them, and invited them to their home, a two-family house with back porches that overlooked a tool and dye factory.

Cousin told Yeshia that work would be his for the asking and Yeshia felt thankful but also doubtful that he could survive hour upon hour of a steady repeated task beneath a roof that shut him in and separated him from sun and air. He thought of himself as a farmer and a fisherman, not an industrial worker. For Leah's sake he went to the factory and for eleven hours a day, six days a week he repeated the same motion over and over again. He thought he'd go insane and yet he found such joy in Leah's happiness as she excelled at school and made friends with the children of the neighborhood.

All of the workers came from the same part of the world as Yeshia and Leah: not the same village, but the same region, a region where national boundaries changed from one war to the next and a region that seemed to be ever at war with itself unlike these miraculous United States. Occasionally, some of the men of socialist leanings printed a paper. The news it contained always referred to events covered by other papers days or weeks before and yet something about the language and its intonation in this paper appealed to Yeshia.

In this erratic paper he read one day about farming communities comprised of people from their region. And so they moved to the nearby state of New Jersey. Leah put up little fuss. She did mention her friends and her school, but Yeshia plied her with the promise of her very own pumpkin patch.

Brotmanville had been founded a few years prior by the industrialist turned philanthropist Ludwig Brotman. He had made his millions in the manufacture of lighting fixtures. Already the settlement had many families from the old country who didn't so much reject the America of industry and commerce as they welcomed that small town nation of happy farmers and bountiful harvests. Yeshia had been granted fifteen acres with the option for fifteen more if all went according to plan.

Yeshia worked like a spinning dervish with pick and ax to clear stumps from this — as he saw it — gift from God that he had received. He refused machinery so that he could cut costs and save and plant and reap. Soon he had a small barn built with his own hands and in his barn he had calves and sheep; a goat, too. And Leah had her pumpkin patch. Once again they had soup and bread, and seeds to snack upon.

But winter comes to this part of the world as it had in their village. Brotman had wisdom as well as great wealth. He built a clothing factory for work in the off-season and all boats were lifted: Brotman's, but also all the families that had settled in Brotmanville.

As new pioneers arrived a new business became a priority and Brotman built a toy factory. To survive the town needed an industrial base as well as the seasonal farms. Unbeknown to Yeshia and Leah, the young man who had befriended the former and delivered a message to the latter had arrived to oversee the beginnings of the new factory. This former soldier now would supervise the manufacture of toy soldiers and dolls and simple board games such as checkers and the little baseball bats and caps made for the nearby Philadelphia team to sell as souvenirs.

The day Leah passed by Velvil along the main thoroughfare they slowed a moment and looked closely but failed to recall why they felt a sense of familiarity. Everyone in Brotmanville came from a similar background and a very limited region within the old country and so everyone could feel a sense of familiarity with anyone else. But the sense they had, the odd feeling that had been roused, they knew differed from the usual acknowledgment of some sort of connection.

A few weeks, perhaps a full month transpired. Then Yeshia passed Velvil on that same street, but unlike his daughter, Yeshia immediately recognized his friend and embraced him. They spoke and Yeshia learned of his friend's escape and learned of his steady and secure work as a supervisor in Brotman's toy factory. And Yeshia told his friend about his daughter, his joy.

Yes, of course, Leah and Velvil married. While Brotmanville was not the old country neither was it quite the new one. Marriages — usually — were not arranged in New Jersey, but bride and groom often selected one another from a very limited applicant pool, a guarded and compact community of the possible.

For Yeshia, America had fulfilled all his desires. Okay, so maybe he had fine fortune after all, but was that only because he also had a deep faith? He felt free and secure now that his daughter had her mate.

The toy factory closed after the birth of their first child but their farm prospered, especially its pumpkin patch, which — as they grew older — became a sort of south Jersey tourist attraction, known for its free hayrides out to the pick-your-own field.

Lift Off

Subject to the contradictions of history, one guides the world to the boundaries separating established symbols from a calendar of prescribed ritual. The stories told set structures on different levels of power. Even those who absorbed the ideology of descent participated in these developments, strands of the same measure. The romantics supplied further division. The center of any proper society relishes the sole inexpressible charm of one side, the only true power. Angry responses cause the conversation to stretch the words of moderates and to relinquish the ideology of active and determined liberals who back the intransigent others. When their concern for many marks a breach in the law of resolution, one can support unexpected ways of concession. And in line with the same spirit of initiative, the editor emphasizes the importance of resolution for the success of leaders. The outcome of competition remains deeply threatened by heated debates that separate our people from a successful order. The life blood of territories protects rather than endorses the pungent restoration of power subject to these remarks on the origin of the world. For the time being. other plans for peace and disarmament will protect the good souls of the imagination from open places. In fact, a powerful force in the imagination has always had an affinity with a vast commemoration for what we think to be a just cause. The most thorough letter to the historians at the banquet surprised businessmen and those unwilling to contribute to our new vision. The events had a twist, so strong that the superiors cooperated. A new generation discerned that traditions in the past could not keep suppressed free speech in the following pages.

THE PURSUIT OF PROPERTY

Don't be misled by the subtitle. This is a lot of reportage and description without the drama of memoir nor the conceptual frame of the monograph. In this city one thousand and one stories have been named but none are told. At the edge of downtown Chicago a band ate leftovers, a solo musician moved into a basement apartment, and all kinds of luggage spoke of infection. In Chicago the custom was to change the beliefs preached, to be a single coherent geography. Still changes began to occur. In the middle of the century it became abandoned, deplored, and no attraction for me. As I reached that point, one person strode forward and others asserted that some would seek to supplement volumes of later concessions. Why does this matter? We had confirmed the slow struggle up and there were many aunts and uncles in the residential quarter. My father moved to Chicago. It would be interesting to know a list of names and arrivals. About six miles from the center, Chicago was nothing but overcrowded. Children played often below street level. Chicago was hard and I saw occasional reference to proud couples, notable lives based on mothers' cherished expectations. In these buildings I visited a laborer for an electric company. Chicago's largest stamped imprint accompanied valentines, letters expressing love. The fact that bells rang out became part of the city. And in Chicago that changed forever the neighborhood, the future. I saw this pattern, but I recall hearing nothing about having any communications with the oldest passengers delayed by the poetry of years.

THAT WAS THE SUMMER

It may well have been a Sunday when I began the long road toward faith. So often the call isn't easy. I was just in the right place for me. I decided to establish some priorities. During all those trials, Jesus defended achievement. I referred to this a few days ago and said, "Our feelings suggested an enormous wall, a skier at the top of the slope." And Thoreau said, "Nature *seems* to set a high standard." Jesus taught there is no substitute for doing a job right. One day a wonderful thing happened. I received a phone call from Jesus. His voice trailed off uncertainly. I told him, "Tell me something important." Worry has never solved a problem. Jesus talked about the same thing. I understood. In a simple everyday situation we are defeated if we believe it can control us. Jesus owned every plane, every flight. Yet, I must have a private room? We never know the day of departure. It's Sunday morning and I imagine every one of us atop a mountain peak. I get up before the sun, prepare to grow with the day. And it works! Jesus spoke after a few minutes. He wanted to slow down and find good in any situation. I had to admit, it is usually a dangerous thing to do. Jesus raised the question: "Can you imagine?" I would figure out a way.

AH, ITALIA!

The worn black sweater is not in a pile of lumber. The cellar is now wide, almost *palazzo*-like. No one listens, no one says, "That's right." They toast the afternoon, two rooms on each side of a hallway. A flock of long-haired sheep seem to be lost. For several years laughter floated over the walls. Once a week, a table draped in white. There is a fountain; olives, chestnuts, and figs; chickens clucking in the yard; the white chicken at the foot of the steps. I have heard it all before. We are safe. Promise. A mule drinks water. Out on the street the earth itself shifts under our feet, a white speck lands on my nose. It's all right. I can feel the letter on the table, the washstand with a bucket of well water; the water tan as dust. A chunk of fresh bread in one hand, I arranged the hills into orchards: that gesture big enough for a dozen years. Half the afternoon was a pin stuck on forever, a black hole in the mind maybe. The closed door told the story, a coat hanger out of the closet. How many years would be lost? The old man, the banker, kept the house, the sheets, and the next time. The immobility of lips in silence. Maybe it was only the time of day, a warning that a mask might remember acts like the crash of that tree. The old man in the boat perceived a mythical place surrounded by water. He stomped around the periphery muttering loudly. I saw fields bursting with wild flowers. Then the lock rattled when we shook it, a vacancy nobody knew existed. People turned and said, "Let's go." The *carabinieri* saluted in our direction. Suddenly, distorted faces anticipated new dangers. We were taken on tough, unsteady land, and then a leaf drifted down, shoved by so many people. And then another face bulged around its bands, the end of the gauze blew in the air like a banner. We glared at the lawyer. And the lawyer said, "I've got to explain." He meant—you're American and from his pocket he took out his handkerchief and got lost around the mound of earth that was once a gun emplacement.

PIRATES

He lives in a house five blocks from hers. His plates clutter the sink; his plates haven't been washed in a week, two weeks, or maybe three. If he opened the door to his front closet in the rat's hole he calls home, an avalanche would explode upon him and might crush him beneath an unused tennis racket, the hook at the end of a line of fishing wire, an old coat brought here a year ago from the colder temperatures and higher elevations of Colorado. You get the idea. If it wasn't for all that loot, they'd might as well move in together, his place or hers.

ERA

My father loved baseball, but he had no sons. He pushed me on to the field and my sisters into the pool or onto the track. He even made a weight room for us in the basement. No one was going to kick sand in the face of one of his daughters. My mom didn't say much until maybe tenth or eleventh grade when we started devoting even more time to our respective sports. I think she worried the three of us would never get married since we never took any time off to go on dates. Our dad often went to my games or my sisters' meets. He'd yell at the umpire like a madman during my games. I began to envy my sister who swam in a pool with googles on and her head down in the water or my other sister who ran cross-country in the fall. Dad didn't know what to make of it. The runners go into the woods and come out fifteen minutes later. Who could he yell at? Who could he egg on? It got so bad for me that I thought about quitting. I took my problems to Rev. Lucy at the Presbyterian Church and that's how — five years later — I ended up in the Peace Corps.

QUESTION AND ANSWER

If I had a brother we would travel together. We would praise God and spread the word. We would set forth and stretch-out mightily the message of hope. We would climb the stairs, board ship, and set sail. Though assigned to different towns, we would continue with the self-same work and we would write about our success. We would write from one to the other, from one city to the other and we would compare but not compete, we would apprise and bless and praise: if I had a brother. But what if this brother with so much skill with words should turn from the Word to numbers? What if he should seek the riches of this world and think less of the spirit and the heavens and the heavenly? And what if he led the bank and increased its holdings; did this work, and gathered more accounts guaranteed in passbooks while I continued to push for conversions, not revenues and returns? It will be the Word and not the jewel that'll grip us; we'll have no need of grand design nor spiral stairs. What nets us can be summoned in silence, and rises, as from death; promises are tendered via clear distinctions circled in prayer. Inside a storefront or beneath the tent's seam, no riches to mirror vanity: some far greater reward will be discovered through tongues present before our beginning.

GOLDEN ANNIVERSARY

There's a car in front of the house. So? Across the street. On the other side. Parked. Old or new? Old. What make? I don't know. What does it look like? It's dark. A dark car with dark windows. Ah, a mobster. Don't be funny. Well, who is in it? I can't tell. I told you, it has dark windows. Get up and take a look for yourself. I'm reading. Put the book down. I really don't care. Why are you reading it then? Not the book. I don't care about the car. What difference does it make if there's a car out front? They could be up to something. They could be casing the joint. Ah, so there's more than one person in the car. I didn't say that. Your pronoun implied as much. It is unusual. The pronoun? No, silly. The car. No one ever parks in front of our house. Sometimes. But not very often. And there is someone now. Yes, and there is someone now and later on there could be someone else. That's true. That's a fact. Though perhaps not a certainty. Who knows? What's that? I said, "Who knows" after you said, "though perhaps not a certainty." No, no. Not that. I mean that noise. The car. Yes, well. What about it? It's gone.

WINTER MUSIC

The white gloves waited in a pile by the front entrance. They weren't assigned to anyone and you grabbed any old pair when you got there. Some of the gloves had begun to yellow and weren't so white anymore. I always tried to pick a bright pair. We used similar gloves in the bell-choir at church but those gloves always sparkled and were never tarnished. I thought it must look strange to see a dozen or so white-gloved people in front of the sanctuary on Sunday mornings. If I had those white gloves now I'd wear them inside my black mittens. It's so damn cold.

FLAT FOOT FAMILY

Our father passed away and left behind meagre comfort as if our house hung in chains. We knew that the ability to stand was up to each and every individual. We had a reverse or two and then took whatever came, an unknown takes every ounce. The railroad came easily to our world: one cold night in a yell of pain. The wheel of fortune we could not let pass and so we were bankrupt in hope. Under a wild rose hedge we'd make grievous complaints. Yet, the light came; conviction grew without seeking reward. A new day came, yes, and the crowd, too, the cave dwellers.

VAST OCULUS

Away from the window there is no searing flash of light. It is enough to stop the blows of the compass. Images upon an inkwell, it is all very confusing and mute resignation accompanies this section, the sunlight and fresh air. At the shop attached to the assembly hall we used to sing with a weary expression anything that made us feel excitement. Another world existed beyond the arm-chair — like the point of a rapier! Yet I was happy and seemed somewhere beyond the horizon. Who knew the tremendous emphasis placed on school? The ditch-digger managed to smile. Away from home I was restless, brooding, and took to wandering the streets. The doctor had gone and I started munching a sandwich. Experience taught us to discuss success, but the words would not come. The idea was that in everything new we have free passage. Once more life in a metropolis existed between excitement and a bored waiting for half that amount, two pages well-translated. What exactly fascinated and tormented children? It was the same old story. Shortly before, we finally got around to an important lesson that could never be bound to money. It was good enough for the outside world. It was as if the church might scheme to stay on with last-minute comments. It was the short-answer type of question and the place upside down. It was the accumulated dead and the boys working longer for a few barrels down in the cellar. This neighborhood of problems and casual talk the beautiful new costumes, the days of tension and struggle. The deciding factor fetched downstairs among salves and dance halls. All this was in addition to those dishes still avoided at lunchtime. See how eager they become? Strike home with the truth, something preying on the mind for a long time. It was here in the new building until late in the evening and the students had walked out in protest. But the crowd and the police and the teachers, everyone had an uneasy feeling that somehow the permanent record would be marked in pencil.

He came without money, which means defeat sometimes. He was, in fact, lean and sickly. Beside his bed, there was a child. He was forced to stay in bed. It was a horrible thing that he had to do: the immobile furniture, the weight of sunken desires, and a sort of silence that happens every day. In every house by the windows the heart remains in the night something wrong as if dust and brushes. There are some flowers on the window sill, a tangle of unmown grass. One fellow goes away from the world, gets up with scattered ash. Another voice says not to fear the truth, to understand the neighbor, the houses, and this land. Don't say, here it is and God-knows that's why and of course! He may dream a sky, a grey mirror over the vault, a whole day at the bottom of laughter, reeds and geraniums. And look, is he going to gesture open-eyed and independent? In the darkness he'll be irresponsible then bewildered by sudden light. And, as if this were not enough, the continual uproar of a blast furnace meddles and nags this damning sentimentality of personal tragedy. He cannot let others talk. He doesn't see sweet words, these features of a face in the air and old worlds meant to be obvious and noisier then any required simplicity, an apology to the admired fine slang of tenderness and hope. But we are not through. Let's open the words themselves, a word moldy and trotting on, anything — the wrangle of sleep and dogma and color, the sky, the utterly impractical necessary. He was born and he has lived a little bit with the emptiness of forgotten inky pens.

The world originated in ferment. Nor was this all. Talk emerged in a pure unadulterated form. There are elements held out to decipher between them a fitting memorial, a spin-off of the true practice. Birds by any standard prospered as a force to contend with until too many years later they became our last resort. Reaching out to the suburbs had managed to be discovered and that welcomed their nests wide. They had no pressing business and would neglect social compromise. In no case was it said that certain food needed to be served; that they eased themselves over monuments and lost count at feasts. What is noticeable between tradition and a lone voice crying against abuse needs to be added to so many perfect gemstones. Let us cast some of this in more sophisticated terms. Elites by and large must be seen as overtures to a creative and decorous order, an assortment of friends. And they mutely support an old esteem for nature but keep community gifts bound to their paper creations. Seen in this context, exalted reason advances enough of us to force all creation toward the very best. To pick a rose works through their efforts nearly all of the hours. Closest of all as a model are the fateful syllables, the generalized ethos of this wood and that holiday. Turn back the dedication and continually use the already-cited names, the best construction that can be made of its marble so violated and brought to our chests. The fields in the first two verses have been a source of great pride for us and the last line may be intentional — a bearer of joy — or simply abandoned for a song.

It is not difficult to know what place makes us examine our remaining books. These works have everything palpable and known, a harmony that makes us forget the incontestable. We leap from the enormous weight and follow ideas without bodies: poetry. Let us then lose the world. Memory holds the rattle and peaceful feelings. A few words become embroidered in thought that should be a nest, a house. If we want to find such spectacles spoiled, then stray from each letter. Everything goes straight to the fireworks when we remember who said suffer horror, nothing positive, whatever. Then bitterness and fear unite in thoughts that start here in front of a better heart, the very best one. We make the spirit, the other roads into shadow; the glow and the fire. We speak of air and the moment igniting. We go into the step that reverberates like white wheels that will never diminish the surface of the day. Under us, this sun and yours too — space, everything, an infinite spin.

MATTERS OF FAITH

I know what I heard; I know what I saw. After the race I walked into the grotto. It really is quite pretty, though this whole town is so picturesque as to be almost unnatural. I don't know why I parked so far away from the start, but I didn't mind jogging downhill after. And in the grotto of all things there was a pay-phone. So I called and said I'd be awhile for I finished third master — pretty good I thought — and so I'd stay to pick-up my prize, two, as it turned out: a Timex sports watch and a rather large, weighty, and impressive sports medal. Vanities of vanity, those trinkets can't compare to what I saw as I wandered in the grotto. After I put the pay-phone back in its proper place, I proceeded to walk around. You may doubt or you may laugh, but it is true. I am not a religious man, perhaps not even especially spiritual, but as I gazed upon Christ on the cross I witnessed a most extraordinary sight. I saw the heartbeat. And I am just the first of many who visited afterwards and witnessed the same pulsing beat. This strange vision cannot be called a mirage of a tired runner, weary with the strained rhythms of his own pulsing heart or the heat of the late afternoon summer sun. They came not only from the monastery to see this spectacle but from the university, too, and science seemed defeated by the undeniable fact of all that the professors could see with their own eyes, touch with their own hands, and test with the many instruments at their disposal. Everything came up pulsing.

VIA FOLIOS
A refereed book series dedicated to the culture of Italians and Italian Americans.

Bordighera Press is an imprint of Bordighera, Incorporated, an independently owned not-for-profit scholarly organization that has no legal affiliation with the University of Central Florida or with The John D. Calandra Italian American Institute, Queens College/CUNY.

RICHARD VETERE. *The Other Colors in a Snow Storm*. Vol. 77. Poetry. $10

GARIBALDI LAPOLLA. *Fire in the Flesh*. Vol. 76 Fiction & Criticism. $25

GEORGE GUIDA. *The Pope Stories*. Vol. 75 Prose. $15

ROBERT VISCUSI. *Ellis Island*. Vol. 74. Poetry. $28

ELENA GIANINI BELOTTI. *The Bitter Taste of Strangers Bread*. Vol. 73. Fiction. $24

PINO APRILE. *Terroni*. Vol. 72. Italian Studies. $20

EMANUEL DI PASQUALE. *Harvest*. Vol. 71. Poetry. $10

ROBERT ZWEIG. *Return to Naples*. Vol. 70. Memoir. $16

AIROS & CAPPELLI. *Guido*. Vol. 69. Italian/American Studies. $12

FRED GARDAPHÉ. *Moustache Pete is Dead! Long Live Moustache Pete!*. Vol. 67. Literature/Oral History. $12

PAOLO RUFFILLI. *Dark Room/Camera oscura*. Vol. 66. Poetry. $11

HELEN BAROLINI. *Crossing the Alps*. Vol. 65. Fiction. $14

COSMO FERRARA. *Profiles of Italian Americans*. Vol. 64. Italian Americana. $16

GIL FAGIANI. *Chianti in Connecticut*. Vol. 63. Poetry. $10

BASSETTI & D'ACQUINO. *Italic Lessons*. Vol. 62. Italian/American Studies. $10

CAVALIERI & PASCARELLI. Eds.. *The Poet's Cookbook*. Vol. 61. Poetry/Recipes. $12

EMANUEL DI PASQUALE. *Siciliana*. Vol. 60. Poetry. $8

NATALIA COSTA. Ed.. *Bufalini*. Vol. 59. Poetry. $18.

RICHARD VETERE. *Baroque*. Vol. 58. Fiction. $18.

LEWIS TURCO. *La Famiglia/The Family*. Vol. 57. Memoir. $15

NICK JAMES MILETI. *The Unscrupulous*. Vol. 56. Humanities. $20

BASSETTI. ACCOLLA. D'AQUINO. *Italici: An Encounter with Piero Bassetti*. Vol. 55. Italian Studies. $8

GIOSE RIMANELLI. *The Three-legged One*. Vol. 54. Fiction. $15

CHARLES KLOPP. *Bele Antiche Stòrie*. Vol. 53. Criticism. $25

JOSEPH RICAPITO. *Second Wave*. Vol. 52. Poetry. $12

GARY MORMINO. *Italians in Florida*. Vol. 51. History. $15

GIANFRANCO ANGELUCCI. *Federico F.*. Vol. 50. Fiction. $15

ANTHONY VALERIO. *The Little Sailor*. Vol. 49. Memoir. $9

ROSS TALARICO. *The Reptilian Interludes*. Vol. 48. Poetry. $15

RACHEL GUIDO DE VRIES. *Teeny Tiny Tino's Fishing Story*. Vol. 47. Children's Literature. $6

EMANUEL DI PASQUALE. *Writing Anew*. Vol. 46. Poetry. $15

MARIA FAMÀ. *Looking For Cover*. Vol. 45. Poetry. $12

ANTHONY VALERIO. *Toni Cade Bambara's One Sicilian Night*. Vol. 44. Poetry. $10

EMANUEL CARNEVALI. Dennis Barone. Ed. *Furnished Rooms*. Vol. 43. Poetry. $14

BRENT ADKINS. et al., Ed. *Shifting Borders. Negotiating Places*. Vol. 42. Proceedings. $18

GEORGE GUIDA. *Low Italian*. Vol. 41. Poetry. $11

GARDAPHÈ, GIORDANO, TAMBURRI. *Introducing Italian Americana*. Vol. 40. Italian/American Studies. $10

DANIELA GIOSEFFI. *Blood Autumn/Autunno di sangue*. Vol. 39. Poetry. $15/$25

FRED MISURELLA. *Lies to Live by*. Vol. 38. Stories. $15

STEVEN BELLUSCIO. *Constructing a Bibliography*. Vol. 37. Italian Americana. $15

ANTHONY JULIAN TAMBURRI, Ed. *Italian Cultural Studies 2002*. Vol. 36. Essays. $18

BEA TUSIANI. *con amore*. Vol. 35. Memoir. $19

FLAVIA BRIZIO-SKOV, Ed. *Reconstructing Societies in the Aftermath of War*. Vol. 34. History. $30

TAMBURRI. et al., Eds. *Italian Cultural Studies 2001*. Vol. 33. Essays. $18

ELIZABETH G. MESSINA, Ed. *In Our Own Voices*. Vol. 32. Italian/American Studies. $25

STANISLAO G. PUGLIESE. *Desperate Inscriptions*. Vol. 31. History. $12

HOSTERT & TAMBURRI, Eds. *Screening Ethnicity*. Vol. 30. Italian/American Culture. $25

G. PARATI & B. LAWTON, Eds. *Italian Cultural Studies*. Vol. 29. Essays. $18

HELEN BAROLINI. *More Italian Hours*. Vol. 28. Fiction. $16

FRANCO NASI, Ed. *Intorno alla Via Emilia*. Vol. 27. Culture. $16

ARTHUR L. CLEMENTS. *The Book of Madness & Love*. Vol. 26. Poetry. $10

JOHN CASEY, et al. *Imagining Humanity*. Vol. 25. Interdisciplinary Studies. $18

ROBERT LIMA. *Sardinia/Sardegna*. Vol. 24. Poetry. $10

DANIELA GIOSEFFI. *Going On*. Vol. 23. Poetry. $10

ROSS TALARICO. *The Journey Home*. Vol. 22. Poetry. $12

EMANUEL DI PASQUALE. *The Silver Lake Love Poems*. Vol. 21. Poetry. $7

JOSEPH TUSIANI. *Ethnicity*. Vol. 20. Poetry. $12

JENNIFER LAGIER. *Second Class Citizen*. Vol. 19. Poetry. $8

FELIX STEFANILE. *The Country of Absence*. Vol. 18. Poetry. $9

PHILIP CANNISTRARO. *Blackshirts*. Vol. 17. History. $12

LUIGI RUSTICHELLI. Ed.. *Seminario sul racconto*. Vol. 16. Narrative. $10

LEWIS TURCO. *Shaking the Family Tree*. Vol. 15. Memoirs. $9

LUIGI RUSTICHELLI, Ed. *Seminario sulla drammaturgia*. Vol. 14. Theater/Essays. $10

FRED GARDAPHÈ. *Moustache Pete is Dead! Long Live Moustache Pete!*. Vol. 13. Oral Literature.
    $10

JONE GAILLARD CORSI. *Il libretto d'autore*. 1860–1930. Vol. 12. Criticism. $17

HELEN BAROLINI. *Chiaroscuro: Essays of Identity*. Vol. 11. Essays. $15

PICARAZZI & FEINSTEIN, Eds. *An African Harlequin in Milan*. Vol. 10. Theater/Essays. $15

JOSEPH RICAPITO. *Florentine Streets & Other Poems*. Vol. 9. Poetry. $9

FRED MISURELLA. *Short Time*. Vol. 8. Novella. $7

NED CONDINI. *Quartettsatz*. Vol. 7. Poetry. $7

ANTHONY JULIAN TAMBURRI, Ed. *Fuori: Essays by Italian/American Lesbians and Gays*. Vol. 6.
    Essays. $10

ANTONIO GRAMSCI. P. Verdicchio. Trans. & Intro. *The Southern Question*. Vol. 5. Social
    Criticism. $5

DANIELA GIOSEFFI. *Word Wounds & Water Flowers*. Vol. 4. Poetry. $8

WILEY FEINSTEIN. *Humility's Deceit: Calvino Reading Ariosto Reading Calvino*. Vol. 3.
    Criticism. $10

PAOLO A. GIORDANO, Ed. *Joseph Tusiani: Poet. Translator. Humanist*. Vol. 2. Criticism. $25

ROBERT VISCUSI. *Oration Upon the Most Recent Death of Christopher Columbus*. Vol. 1. Poetry.
    $3